IT'S TIME TO EAT CHICKEN FRIES

It's Time to Eat
CHICKEN FRIES

Walter the Educator

Silent King Books
A WhichHead Entertainment Imprint

Copyright © 2025 by Walter the Educator

All rights reserved. No part of this book may be reproduced in any manner whatsoever without written per- mission except in the case of brief quotations embodied in critical articles and reviews.

First Printing, 2024

Disclaimer

This book is a literary work; the story is not about specific persons, locations, situations, and/or circumstances unless mentioned in a historical context. Any resemblance to real persons, locations, situations, and/or circumstances is coincidental. This book is for entertainment and informational purposes only. The author and publisher offer this information without warranties expressed or implied. No matter the grounds, neither the author nor the publisher will be accountable for any losses, injuries, or other damages caused by the reader's use of this book. The use of this book acknowledges an understanding and acceptance of this disclaimer.

It's Time to Eat CHICKEN FRIES is a collectible early learning book by Walter the Educator suitable for all ages belonging to Walter the Educator's Time to Eat Book Series. Collect more books at WaltertheEducator.com

USE THE EXTRA SPACE TO TAKE NOTES AND DOCUMENT YOUR MEMORIES

CHICKEN FRIES

It's time to eat, oh what a treat,

It's Time to Eat
Chicken Fries

Something crispy, something neat!

Golden sticks, all in a line,

Chicken Fries, they're so divine!

Dip them here, dip them there,

In some ketchup if you dare.

Barbecue or honey sweet,

Every dip is fun to eat!

Crunchy, munchy, in my hand,

Tasty fries so very grand.

Made of chicken, not a fry,

But they're yummy, oh my my!

Line them up or make a shape,

Like a star or silly grape.

Chicken Fries can play before,

You crunch and munch and ask for more!

It's Time to Eat
Chicken Fries

Circle sauce cups all around,

Dip and dip, then hear the sound.

Crunch, crunch, munch, munch,

Chicken Fries are fun to crunch!

Snack time, lunch time, any day,

Chicken Fries love to play.

With some apples, or some cheese,

Eat them up, they aim to please!

Count them out, one, two, three,

Then eat them up, Yippee, Yippee!

Chicken Fries are here to stay,

Yummy fun in every way.

Pass the plate, we'll share a few,

For me and also some for you!

Dipping, crunching, laughing too,

It's Time to Eat
Chicken Fries

Chicken Fries for me and you!

When they're gone, we say "All done!"

Eating Chicken Fries is fun.

Next time, maybe, we will try,

Chicken Fries with apple pie!

Now we clean and wipe our hands,

Chicken Fries were so grand.

Thank you fries, you were so sweet,

It's Time to Eat
Chicken Fries

Tomorrow we'll have more to eat!

ABOUT THE CREATOR

Walter the Educator is one of the pseudonyms for Walter Anderson. Formally educated in Chemistry, Business, and Education, he is an educator, an author, a diverse entrepreneur, and he is the son of a disabled war veteran. "Walter the Educator" shares his time between educating and creating. He holds interests and owns several creative projects that entertain, enlighten, enhance, and educate, hoping to inspire and motivate you. Follow, find new works, and stay up to date with Walter the Educator™

at WaltertheEducator.com

www.ingramcontent.com/pod-product-compliance
Lightning Source LLC
LaVergne TN
LVHW052011060526
838201LV00059B/3965